EXPECTING DELAYS

George Bishop

FUTURECYCLE PRESS
Mineral Bluff, Georgia

Copyright © 2013 George Bishop
All Rights Reserved

Published by FutureCycle Press
Mineral Bluff, Georgia, USA

ISBN 978-1-938853-19-7

Contents

Sunday	9
Expecting Delays	10
Timing	11
Riding by Anthony's	12
Passing on Grace	13
Causalities	14
Two Separate Incidents	16
Labels	17
Renewing Something	18
After Walking the Dog	19
Faithfulness	20
On Telling Stories More Than Once	21
Fish Story	22
Knees	23
Almost Home	24
Finished	25
Meditations by an Old Bridge	26
Backhoe	27
Finding My Grandmother	28
Passage	29
Strange Stories	30
Hearts	31
The Caretaker's House	32
Cedars, 1880	33
Working the Garden One Night	34
Initials	35
Thinking of You From a Canoe	36
Statistics	37
Flight	38
Toast	39
Behind Me	40
Fitting Rooms	41
Climbing the Stairs of an Old Hotel	42
The Man in the Orange Cap	43
Suicide	44

An Empty House	45
Early Edition	46
In My Other Glasses	47
The Children	48
What's Inside	49
Child Reaching for Maps	50
Primitives	51
Bonnie Lee's	52
Downtown Deciding on a Movie	53
Last Courthouse Hanging	54
Weathervane	55
Clouds and Sun	56
Daily Gods	57
Staying Inside	58
Shadowing	59
Signs	60
Gospel	61
Answering the Question	62
The Sky and I	63
Watching Dolphins in the Harbor with the Homeless	64
Home	65
Inlet	66
Current	67
After Test Results	68
Acknowledgments	69

*Nothing can travel at the speed of light, they say,
forgetful of the shadow's speed.*

—Howard Nemerov

To Chris Meyers

8 EXPECTING DELAYS

Sunday

Bad day for buzzards.
I can tell by the way they sit
in separate trees, on different billboards,
breathing the death-empty air.
Not concerned with any other kind
of peace, black with patience, they know
the sky is the wrong place to expect
to be heard. For now, they circle inside
themselves, used to the half-prayer, half-
answer world—resting in the mathematics
of this life and the next.

Expecting Delays

I'm taking a train into myself today, sitting
in a reserved seat reserved for someone else.

The only stops are unscheduled, departures
all, arrivals an unstable solution of disguise

and similitude. Between cars the chaos is lover-
like, iron sparked madness, directions hopeless—

doubtless a scene in one of my many sleepers
not far away. I'm on time because I'm not

being timed, passing ties soaked in creosote
and buried in ballast packing, feeling the rails

feeling for themselves. The rust is relentless
as the whistle that won't quit—up ahead

things are waiting to cross but they'll have
to wait. The window won't allow me to leave,

my glassy face looking in at the emptiness
sitting in the other seat, checking the watch

I can't read against the sky it can't see, hands
coming apart like unusable track as we go.

Timing

on Ruby at Broadway

Twice a day the clock above
a bankrupt insurance company

is correct. I hope it's never fixed—
it reminds me of all the 6:44s

that have gone by unnoticed.
I can't even remember having

to be anywhere at that time
until now. I come here often,

early, even though time stopped
and never turned back. I gaze down

into digits lit up on my wrist, wonder
who might've been looking up when

the huge hands quit working,
began pointing to a different

face—perhaps it was an ancient sun-
dial deep in someone's soul, stone

announcing only space can save
him and only from himself.

Riding by Anthony's

Even in a house handed him
he wanted more. It wasn't a home,
and never would be, the septic small,
the kitchen a place to be alone.
He was his own neighbor, knew it
all. His mother, grandmother and step-
father wouldn't die fast enough,
and he, a father, knew time had moved
most of its things elsewhere, leaving
no forwarding address, taking away
what might've worked for him.
He often found himself beating his
head against the walls of his son,

everything before his eyes and in them
turning to toys. The woman, who
only goes by *the boy's mother*, comes
and goes. Homeless herself, that
in-between-lives look is so hard
to hide. A monastic feel, nothing
belongs to anyone—unanswered
prayers all day, unheard prayers
all night. And in between a house
handed him, church-empty, I say,
no place for beggars, where ghosts
of the rich go mirror to mirror
looking for a way out.

Passing on Grace

The word and the act at dinner became unclear—
the goodwill of allowing everyone equal portions

seemed more meaty, the secret recipe of something-
battered fish closer to the prayer we all prayed

differently. If you kept yours open you could watch
each eye making corrections beneath lightly veined

lids, weighing something, spices maybe. Once, over
dessert, someone even asked me if I believed God

could change His mind—ghost-quick I began
sniffing through my bible backyards where the dog

inside has always buried such bones. *Not sure,*
I told him without telling him as he told me

he wasn't sure what he meant, passed on grace,
said some things could've been better. I wanted

to know what they were but knew translations
are all that reach us, hearsay our hidden selves

speak. A god-nod filled my heart like a well-
deserved belch, heaven moving away in perfect

circles of empty plates. Breakfast soon, eggs up
making more perfect circles, and there's obedience

at a cave wall painting fire to stone, blowing it
for words. Praise the birds in the morning, all

the sounds they have for light, all the light
in their sounds. Amen.

Causalities

> *Every black hole contains a new universe.*
> —Fox News

One afternoon waves arched into jets
lifting off dark runways, marooning

my inner eyes on stretches of sand
so desolate the shells spoke freely,

dropped their ocean codes and coasted
to the calm back bays of each ear—

I heard the lost language my mother's
womb once spoke, felt the safety

I didn't know was safety, the trans-
parent not-as-deep space of a second

child who knows what he's exploring
has been hunted before. I was away

from systems of reward and punishment
that nightly fool and fade, the weather

of reason moving from time zone to time
zone, always away from mine. I became

a universe in a universe in the black hole
of a *Parent Universe*—it's what the article

suggested, the rotation of *Parent* pulling
me closer to possibilities. This parallel place

is only open to sleep and only for so long—
the cold whistle of a lifeguard woke me,

said someone's out too far, beyond the bar
where it drops off and light curves through

the sea. Another rescue that's impossible
to prove, salvation out of answers again.

I let the magic of doubt work on the absence
of accuracy—the waves are signals, now,

soaked in static, divinations too deep to reach.
I'm happily out of touch and loving this space

between things—holes in the dark, perfect
shapes for faith to soar, become my own.

Two Separate Incidents

The squirrels are especially edgy this morning,
nerves needling the end of each hair—everything's
so stunning. The speed of the wind changing, a cloud
passing, the sudden disappearance of a shadow—
I'm thinking some quotas are out of reach;
even their eyes have begun to look like nuts—
not enough nuts, not enough nuts, their gaping
mouths seem to say. Their order is always nuts,
then survive, and this morning one squirrel took
the rule too far, went out on the wrong limb.
It was no cloud and there weren't enough nerves—
A goshawk was only a few branches above him

looking like the self portrait of a god just painted
with a razor. Death never looked so good.
If squirrels could make comparisons, this end
would sure beat dying in the wheel well of a Coup
de Ville, a flock of crows watching from a wire.
At my desk on the other side of the window
I studied the circle of life getting smaller, knowing
I was his only hope, knowing hope is desire
on its best behavior, that if I was aware of how
close desperation sleeps to me I'd be edgy too, change
the order of a few things. I'd say it was over quick
but everything's over quick, just not quick enough.

Labels

I've been waiting for the scent of wild
honeysuckle to fill the air for over an hour,
long enough for a pool of wax to form
in the center of the candle. I'm beginning
to feel like the flame, working my way
down the wick in search of something
to change my mood, hoping the image
on the glass will invite me in—a vine
weaving through a farmer's rusted fence,

then deep into a harvest night, his wife
barely enduring the hours alone. Later,
still no scent. No farmer. No fence.
Just me, a mood and a dollar's worth
of dim light. It seems fair. The farmer's
wife's still around, honeysuckle somewhere.
She leaning out a window, taking a deep
breath while I dream the wax hard, curl
the wick, let the smoke lead me away.

Renewing Something

The man with one leg is taking his evening walk, passing
the pawn shop where several normally lit letters are dark,
reminding me of the gold-chain watch I secretly sold there—
a gift to my ex-wife from her grandmother many years ago.
Even regret wouldn't touch that one, forgiveness far away
as gold from a dead prospector. That secret never stood
a chance even though tide after tide of alcohol assured me
my tracks were covered. I went to sea in myself after that,

most days drifting on a raft of better moments, sky-stunned.
You'd think it would always be night in me, but daylight
knows how good I am at shadows, how good they are at me.
The man with one leg is gone, now, his cold metal crutches
having taken me back to the beer I used to hide in the snow.
The pawn shop's about to close—a part of me still standing
at the counter signing something, asking for more time,
promising to be back, one foot in front of the other.

After Walking the Dog

We stare at one another
after we come home,
roll on our secret carpets,
and sniff the air for what
followed us back. There's
things we want to dig up
next time, others we need
to bury. Each night we sleep
closer to our bones, names
and places cooling together
at the end of each claw.

Faithfulness

on the death of a friend

He would joke with squirrels
in the morning, forgive raccoons.
He'd slow dance into the eyes of deer
while they nibbled berries each winter—
listening to the litanies of snow
as it warmed the earth.

However, when it came to his dog,
True, prayer turned inward, home
fires were out of control, demands
deeper than a dog could dig—the leash
he didn't believe in was unbreakable.

The dog obeyed. Always. I wondered
about that, what happens when faith
ends, begins that long walk back
through different cures, other masters
lighting the way with sounds even he
couldn't hear. Poor dog. So good

at what he didn't do, the recurring
nightmare of running in his sleep
never far from his fur, the fur
his owner never touched with anything
except the fear of what's faithful.

On Telling Stories More Than Once

for a Black Swallowtail

He'd seen as much as he wanted to see—
the fast life of a caterpillar had caught up

with him. Now, he cursed the chrysalis
for his color, the dragonfly for its control,

the air for all its sudden moves. Just once
he wished his wings would fall off when

he stopped—he wanted to blend again,
inch away. Direction was hopeless—

rescued by an instinct he didn't know was his,
he'd been lured to flowers without knowing

why, learned to hate the sound of the wind,
had begun to reject the whole idea of being

born again. He even chose a sidewalk to halt
his hereafter, deciding not everyone's fit for

resurrection—death can be just what you need
when you want to go on without wings.

Fish Story

The strength of his right side was drawn
into the milk of infancy, the true stories

lost somewhere on his tongue—his best
fishing was done with his eyes anymore

after a stroke rewrote his prayers. Still,
he knew the value of keeping light away

from water, to let the gears of his reel
and the tightening of a knot give orders.

His face showed no sign of weakness
when a hook had to be set—he'd learned

to catch something in his half smile
was to let something else get away.

Knees

Wakulla Springs, one summer

Some say they help the cypress breathe easier
during the rainy season, act as an alternate

exchange of air, get things out down closer
to the root. I can't remember the last time

I prayed on my knees but I must've been
desperate, it had to be unplanned, so wholly

selfish the first god to come through would do.
And I'm still capable of crawling if necessary,

dirtying some imaginary path. I came here
today repenting but the spring isn't aware

of what I'm talking about, keeps cleansing itself.
At the lodge a list of what wasn't answered

quite right hangs like a nest of wasps. *I wish
there would've been a warning,* I thought, a sign.

We only go down so far for what we believe
is necessary—we hold our breath, take it

anyway. For us, seasons are optional, little
changes as they open and close—bend, lean

into one another, form the years we try to call
back, short of breath, full of avidity and mirage.

Almost Home

Nothing except the sound of the house—
clocks at work clearing their throats,

always behind, half a cup of coffee
still awake, staining what we left unsaid,

and certain kitchen air hiding
deep in the face of a spoon.

The cat wants something or nothing,
and a fly in the window's stunned

by what's not in the window. Maybe
I'm just looking too far ahead,

undressing what's coming up the stairs
after hearing a secret knock at every door,

undressing as it comes—there's bound to be
something missing after it finds me.

After all, I've been here the whole time,
straightening the picture of my mother

while the picture of my father straightens
a picture of me. I'm thinking I should

write to my sister, the other only child
who's listening from another room, pivoting.

It's been a long time since we've all
been this close.

Finished

for George Bishop, 1889

Like my great uncle George
after a day of duck hunting,
planting the butt of a shotgun
on shore to steady himself,
step out, I find my mind scattered
across the surface of a lake,
the air empty, reason somewhere
between the sky and the sky.
Nothing gray listens long
before it falls into itself,
but there's not even a storm
due, there's more rain in fog,
thunder in the unspent shells
of a quiet day alone, distant.

Of course, my great uncle couldn't
gather his thoughts at the end
of that day. His blood simply mingled
with that of a few ducks in the boat
that decided not to fly past, maybe
the oars still in the water, finished.
I don't know. I wasn't born yet.
The details died with relatives
who took me no further than
the sound no one heard. However,
I must've heard something for this man
I never met to appear on overcast days,
to come ashore with my name,
steady himself.

Meditations by an Old Bridge

Just a few supports left looking
like big, broken pencils stuck in
a cedar creek—and I can't help
but think about the last train crossing,
a clock stopping at each station,

the silence of the next morning.
I'm sure what goes unnoticed
was watching that day behind
some ancient illusion, waiting
for the earth to shake, the hiss
of steam and scream of a whistle.

Instead, the sound of empty churches
must've risen through the trees,
prayers burning off. The sun likely
began pulling rails right away, rust
spreading its plans for the next rain.

The sky still poles the copper water,
the water darkens the sky—both
have been bridges long enough
to know schedules are only good
for timing their own death, a way
for some next thing to arrive.

Backhoe

William, 1885-1951

My grandfather imagined an assembly line
when he was dying—the shovel, boom and plow
all coming together in the sour air of his hospital
room. He saw the whole thing traveling all night
on a flatbed, the cab cold and dark. He knew
the operator was having a beer somewhere else,
describing the new design to friends, the bucket's
ability to lay the earth evenly as he backfilled,

no mechanical spasms, no hydraulic seizures.

And one morning there it was, off to the side—
a brand new Caterpillar with a quiet attitude, idling,
gears ready to move smooth as ghosts in a mirror.
Grandfather hovered over the hole so deep in his coffin
parts of his life were out of reach no matter how far
our tears fell. And later we talked about how good
he was at making things fit, always insisting it's never
a new day, just the same one reshaping itself.

Finding My Grandmother

dead. All that's left of her is age
and the open windows of her eyes.
They say sight's the first to go
when you're dying, which means
the last frame of your life is frozen
and there's a chance you have
a brief moment to hold it up to

whatever light's still lit—maybe
hope someone like me comes along
and gently takes it from you
like a postcard that keeps being
returned. Your version of the world,
the world it lived in, and a message
too long to repeat.

Passage

It was the perfect day to sit motionless
in the cemetery with the dead, my favorite
bench between Shorn and Bliss empty.
There was just enough morning mist to

give the graves a lively look. You could feel
the wind taking a deep breath before deciding

on a direction, sense the silence slowly washing
the names away as if the stone were a sandy beach

and I combing the edges, sifting for some evidence
of myself. Almost perfect, I should say—the water

waiting in sprinklers, timed and set to splash across
blankets and grass, a nightlight living out its last few

moments. Best suit and bones beneath my feet,
I walk away one winter at a time, thoughts

vanishing in the gears of a backhoe, the sounds
they make and the sounds they don't.

Strange Stories

I didn't want one before bed when I was small.
Not then. Not now. Just the presence of one,
a room wallpapered with possibilities. I wanted
my mother's silence, her hands folded across
her lap, the end of the dark hall full of her eyes—
I know now they were trying to read the lips
of a stranger, a scout of Alzheimer's who'd cut
her key and come in. He wouldn't leave without
her and her stories, especially how much she
hated the family dog. She'd tell the one about
me over and over when my name came up—
I have a son! she'd say, as if there might be
other endings. It's something I'll never forget.

Hearts

There's a dark spot on her heart.
             —The doctors

They have to go in. Nothing's clear enough from
the outside. It's not the usual dark of the heart.
They can guess but they don't or they do in silence,
talk about it later with a wife, a girlfriend or both,
someone skilled in the art of identification, whose nod
is enough for the kind of solace they seek. What's our
own without a name isn't easy to remove, and far away
in a heart that doesn't need to beat for nourishment
she seems to wonder whether to go or stay—she bathes
in the ebb and flow of a self-centeredness that's saved her
for so long. She knows guilt's found its way out of her
desires but suspects it's begun to find a way back.
So we speak to her from something without muscle
or duty, letting personal remedies fail, the anesthesia

of our daily lives dilute in her pillow of half-sleep.
Tonight we'll think of other light passing through
us, how it forms shadows that look everywhere
for something warm and clock-like. We'll pray
no one finds what we've hidden one day, names it.
We'll wonder what her dark spot will be tomorrow.
Taking something from what's hard and set in its ways
can be tricky. I wanted to tell her if something goes
wrong (right) she'll be surprised who was saved,
even more surprised by what they were saved from—
but I didn't. It's too close to the heart. Someone needs
to go in with the steadiness of a stranger, someone
who's been in the dark before and emerged without one
bloody reason to return, not a single shadow in sight.

The Caretaker's House

circa 1920

The responsibilities of an ax and arm,
a hatchet and hand had to be enormous.
The sleep of a caretaker had to leave
little room for dreams—someone else's
job. Without a weed eater, chain saw,
leaf blower, even without a decent rake
care must've meant something other
than brushing back the hair of a stranger
in a hospice, more than watching yourself
slip out of your own mother's memory
moment by moment. I even wonder if
anyone bothered with edges, what
topiaries were thinking deep in hedges—
hiding, hoping no one would find the wrong
face. And the house itself, fashioned for
the homeless, nothing there to call your own
except the air. Which is why I think he'll
like it here walking between the lines
of the same day, looking up at the little title
now and then, going back to the beginning,
each hand in the shape of a different handle.

Cedars, 1880

One by one they fell, bull-drug down
the creek, cracker whips electric as the eyes
that guided them. But both ends of the brackish
waterway turn to swamp now—things fan out

like blood on a back road after a deer's been hit.
Floating anything to the mill ended when gator
nests appeared and the soggy beds of mosquitoes
began to move their desires of soft skin around.

On a clear night you could hear talk of disease,
of things that come out at night looking like bark.
A few years and orange groves took over, cheap
labor and a new roof over an old packing house.

The buzzards are still around. They know the more
things move the more they won't. They know
we're made up of stars and how things burn out.
A shingle and lathe company years ago—the name

stuck. Shingle Creek then, Shingle Creek now.
Wetlands. Protected. No trespassing after five
but it's too late. We've been there, left our rusted
parts behind—can't make a thing out of beauty.

Working the Garden One Night

I left my gloves and spade in the shed,
wore my good jeans and new, cotton,
white shirt—starched, ready to impress.
Photosynthesis on break, a sign hangs
in the shadow of a tree—*Back at dawn.*

What grows goes underground at night,
which is where I go, catching weeds by
surprise, working with manure worms
and dung beetles like a full moon, giving
the earth some air. It reminds me of my
father in his grave, the father who loved
fishing—fresh bait and blitz before a

storm. As for me, I like to keep things
a prayer away and believe in the dirt
of impossibilities. I keep an open pack
of seeds in my top pocket while I work,
planting each distance to a lost relative

too deep. The seeds stay. I water them
well with my lack of sleep, keep any idea
of germination cold and out of reach.
Like the sun, I'm always feeling for
some luck, following the rain around
like a fisherman looking for a hole—
before I know it, the sign is gone.

Initials

I don't see them much anymore.
Maybe there aren't enough rooms

in initials or perhaps it just takes
too long to carve a heart. I find

a stump to do deep thinking anymore—
weight promises. Sometimes, I sit

spitting shells of sunflower seeds
and dream of an attic with chopped

oak beams, an old mirror
and the perfect dust.

Thinking of You From a Canoe

for C. F.

Paddling Shingle Creek,
the banks of southern oaks
and cedar tipping my mind
toward the next bend, a tinge
of prehistoric silence is still
in the air, a vestige of crude
instinct foraging the underbrush,
a banished lover with a plan.
The nakedness of each unseen eye
holds fast against my intrusion,
each behind a veil of deception
designed by some endless network
of light and dark. The otter alters
between a world of air and one
of water, the woodpecker works
from dead tree to dead tree—
diversions all. I sink into
the brackish arena afraid
to look back, to look down,
struggling with the drapes
of Spanish moss.

Statistics

for Jay Chase

You told me your marriage was ending after twenty-three years
and I told you marriage is made up of unfinished sentences—
perhaps one day she'll remember something about your life
insurance or how you went to bed naked and loved the thrill
of being a volunteer fireman. Then, there's that depressed
neighborhood her mind's renamed for the father she never knew,
where you found yourself being called with the wrong equipment.

This time you're in the company of strangers she hasn't met but will.
And when other men appear, as they surely will, you must remember
the way she could make other women yours and how you praised her
for the precision of their work. It's sad. It's always sad seeing these
things end the same way they began, explanations that need explaining,
the need that never explains anything—like separate sides of a bed,
so close we have to leave through different doors, by our own clock.

Flight

Two balloons dyed circus colors were making
the morning light deceptively full, the way to work
suspicious. The issues waiting were well grounded,
still packed in the ice of a restless night. The radio
kept insisting this, then that—I sensed the humid
air beyond the steamed windows holding the balloons
up, making them appear motionless, quiet as clouds

when the wind's ready to change. You don't follow
them the way you do some top-secret launch, a comet
about to disappear for another thousand years. This is
rainbow-driven, distance emptying each basket, nothing
there but the part of you that walked out on your wife,
the ropes you cut swaying like ribbons in your blood-
shot eyes, the weights you saved hugging the sky.

Toast

I've always insisted a toast
be performed with just one glass
ever since my divorce came together—

you know, that sensation of, say,
a bus drifting back, your mind
still moving forward, body at ease

until the departure stuns the eye,
tricks you. That's what falling
out of love feels like someone once

told me. Yes, one glass. No
ting of temporary goodwill,
no collision of separate crystal—

just some sweet breath pulling
the wine past a pair of lips,
one lover at a time—

you making sure to drink last,
someone else wondering
if you've taken too much

and both breaking other glasses
against two new beds
of rekindled coal.

Behind Me

She had heels meant to be heard and drove them
through the wooden floors like an ax, smiling
as they dug through laptops, paperbacks and long
stares. The coffee shop had become a stage,
and I tried to imagine her face as she passed—
the cut of her mouth, the extra-hold of her hair,
the thought of espresso expressing itself in her hips.
It's hard for such a step to hide—our backs catch
what our eyes miss sometimes. After she leaves
the air continues to speak of her. We listen—adjust
our fingertips on keyboards, skip a few pages, turn
to a different window. Our names are almost on our
lips again, the ones we know and the ones she gave us.

Fitting Rooms

for you

Once the door that hides little is locked,
all the thieves that can fit in a mirror have

found you—before you find the glass
or even dress for your imaginary catwalk,

they're already taking turns turning
when you turn, testing their piercing

stare and perfect posture. It's too late
for your eyes, which makes it too late

for everything else—even if it's not
you, it's you.

Climbing the Stairs of an Old Hotel

This was no hotel—not then, certainly not now. The freight elevator, the only elevator, says so. So—I take the stairs.

At each landing I sense the fire door opening without opening. Something's always following you, but this is

different, like dormant genes taking shape, looking to make some changes. I'm sure. Sure as I was when I declined

the elevator opening in the lobby like the toothless mouth of an old man coming in and out of a coma. Sixth floor—

the last floor. The halls speak of truckage, other traffic patterns. The door's already open when I reach the room.

Out of breath, I notice how bright the lights are through the crack, that the indoor-outdoor carpet is mostly outdoor,

pieced together like neighborhoods on a city map no longer safe. As I try to imagine where the continental breakfast

might've been prepared, I realize it's been years since I felt this at home this far from home, happy room service is dead,

overwhelmed that there is no chance in hell for a wakeup call. I'll sleep. Dream of taking the elevator just once. Just once.

The Man in the Orange Cap

He didn't know
I knew about his loss—
that he brought her here
for breakfast each week,
that she died on Halloween.
And here it is,
the season again.
The servers know
to leave him alone
when his last coffee comes,
not to touch the plate
with the crust of light
toast in the shape
of a heart. I can't help
but want to know
the name he wrote
in the egg yolk
with a toothpick,
why he stayed
until it hardened
like a freshly poured
sidewalk.

Suicide

for Paul and Paul

I didn't know it was a different Paul at first and a word like that
whispered, standing alone, is an awful body of images you can't

remove. Your impulse is to keep them coming at any cost—
familiar blood in a backyard seeping into the ground, an empty

bottle of pills near a nightstand, directions for most anything now.
I even imagined a garden hose in his garage taped through a crack

in a car window, everything out of gas. For fifteen minutes Paul
was dead. And then he wasn't. The relief of a stranger passing on

instead swept over me like a magician's silk scarf. I was as close
to my version of the unexplained as I wanted to be. No. Just close.

I could feel faith's cold magnet coming from—inside? More relief.
Then my soul's applause died down. I wanted to say I was ashamed

of the speechless duet I'd just performed, death and joy dancing
naked in my head. However, shame always feels safe in silence.

I believe I uttered some small prayer for the deceased before moving
on. I think—the suicide had just blended in after being filled with

so many illusions. I never noticed it exit through the mirror where
I stood forgiving myself, the one hanging off one of my remote stage

doors. I was thinking of all the times I'd mistaken myself for someone
I didn't know. It was as if nothing had happened, then happened again.

An Empty House

sits quietly
along the widened road
just a few feet from the street—
the hollow gaze of storm windows
and the silence of crumbling wicker
have made this home for whatever's
homeless in me. The freshly poured
concrete curb hardens without a gap
for the overgrown driveway, extending
past the property lines, the untrimmed
hedges and tiny utility flags. The owners
are gone, have taken the curtains. No trace
of children or a dog—just the steel
bones for a few chain stores on both
sides, coming together—surveyors
hold their arms in the air like wands,
a pair of unfinished gods getting
a few things straight.

Early Edition

The paper girl's late again so I have to wait,
the news and I getting older together, apart,
the way it was when everything happened. Already
things have changed, and by the time I find the eye,
hurricane Someone will be clear about the beach,
its picturing, how it wants things—perhaps a person
of interest has been found a few blocks away. I turn
to yesterday's paper, the lead story short of oil, a fire
out, a wedding over—Baumiller and Gorby still dead
as they were when they were alive. Maybe this is
what I need, to read a few articles over, find out
where the words settled. They open up in you like
today's paper, the one the dog brought in when
I wasn't looking, while I watched the neighbor's
wife leave in a hurry, dark glasses on before dawn,
a suitcase deep in her purse. I'm thinking tears,
maybe something swollen, bruises coming together.

In My Other Glasses

Prescription-proof—not the lenses I look through
all day and night. Self-cleaning—unlike what I wear

here, streaked with ancestors, focused on shattered
fortunes. If only I could remember where I left them,

or maybe they fell off my face as I was being born,
the face my family imagined during those dark months

when there was nothing to see—rims made of my father's
secret love, the glass of my mother's tears separating

the worlds we populated. And then the parent in me
became a parent and they appeared pushed up on my

daughter's head, reading the sky to her mind, keeping
the same things from her they kept from me—nothing

like looking through, if you could look through, see
something so complete it wouldn't die of your name.

The Children

chase fireflies like bats on a hospital lawn
grown dark, while inside older children stare

through x-rays, rooms away from a loved one.
Something's spread. The doctors say they'd

be taking the patient out of the illness now—
the illness would live for awhile, they say

to themselves. The children play near
a retention pond, the surface smooth as

the glass of water by their grandfather's bed,
his pills still as stones the children are

sure to find and try to throw the furthest.
The stones go further than they know.

A decision's been made and like all decisions
no one can live with it, not fully. Secretly

they must make changes and do. On the way
home each child is lost in the aerodynamics

of the evening, tailing hard questions—
wondering if the age of a soul has anything

to do with distance—the younger ones out loud
in their sleep, the older to themselves still awake.

What's Inside

to a grandchild

I love when the look of wonder on your face
as you open a gift, when the moment's puzzling,

suddenly missing a piece. The look was there
when you opened a fishing pole I gave you, the one

I knew you'd likely never use. Not alone anyway.
I could hear you questioning the shape of each lure,

casting each one as far as their color would go.
I could see you studying the steel of a hook,

stopping at the tip while your fingers played out
the lives of plastic worms wriggling in the air.

I could picture you when you're old, changing
lines that never got wet—wondering what you

might've caught, weighing things that got away—
like love and the gifts we left unopened.

Child Reaching for Maps

She was three, maybe four years old, ages away
from maps and schedules, timers set to govern
how late or lost she'd become, how partially found
amid hours that would go by dark and undiscovered.

However, excess was already active, had her reaching
for stacks of bus routes. They could've been anything—
directions to a famous battlefield, a deathbed worth
remembering, maybe a theme park's colorful gardens.

How I long for the single, intense eye of her arrivals—
it reminds me how I once loved appearing to my parents
as a solitary thought, a balloon crossing their radar-days,
some part of an unidentified secret closing in on them.

I want to look down again from a basket still warm as
my mother's breasts, feel the original map of myself.
The little girl left with both hands full, enough to declare
some small independence, to begin to pave and widen.

Primitives

Passing aisles of antiques
nothing lures me like primitives—
something fought off, absolution
from certain air and the course
finish of abandoned success.
There's a Victorian sewing bird,
a Shaker berry pail and faded
butterfly quilt. In the distance
a pair of church dolls look up
out of a sleigh in dusty dresses
waiting for what they outlived—
their eyes still forbidden
and the wish of lips sewn
somewhere deep inside.

Bonnie Lee's

Once it was a service station
and I'm eating in what used to be

the left bay. Before that it was
probably a farm where everyone

got to know themselves better than
they should. If I dug deep enough

I'm sure I'd find an oil pit, a rusted
sickle. If I sat long enough I could

watch the smile of the waitress
disappear and the cook come

through the kitchen door wiping
his hands on a dirty cloth.

On my way out I decide
everything was probably once

a farm with a house at the end
of a gravel road. The highway

went through a few years back
and the children had to learn

to fall asleep to the thunder
of trucks, while men in rockers

picked out repairs like planets
on a cold, clear night.

Downtown Deciding on a Movie

I stop at a window where bronze sundials sit like old men
on a park bench. Without some sort of light the best compass
begins to guess, sometimes lie, and these were no exception
as they read by the dim glow of vintage table lamps shrouded
in stained glass. They've been arguing since they were displayed
together in a half circle—how much time is left, if something's
early or late, the effectiveness of on-time arrivals, dismissing

the value of departures. And soon my reflection decides it's seen
enough and I cancel the movie, move on, bring home bronze
thoughts and the small touches of electrolysis. I forget the differences
of clocks and lean back in a rocker that rocks to the beat of my
grandfather's heart when it beat, close my eyes. The sundials have
reminded me time is always right without reminding me—it's hands
that keep fooling me, desperate to make it their own. They can't stop.

Last Courthouse Hanging

for Eddie Broom, January 1912

It was time
for things to fall.
Early October. Halloween
had begun to take off its mask,
knock on some doors. The usual
answers. Agreement in great numbers—
scary, something headless in us all,
our faith in hoods rising from a few
graves. The stairs are still there,
the courthouse a landmark. No more
decisions. Sometimes it only takes
one. A cold snap and a Christmas
pageant appears on the lawn where
townsfolk watched Eddie hang.
Familiar music. Better at night.

Weathervane

Heading southeast
it finally refused
the other winds,
not even the slightest
departure—without notice
the carriage bogged down
in a bed of rust, the driver
and his horse beginning
to chip and gray.

No more
the sharp turns
of sky, the idea
of dodging a star
or dealing with the
act of a god—the last
message it received
was off the sea,
laced in salt—
some voices
going down,
something else
rising, mounting
the backs of rain.

Clouds and Sun

He'd already decided on gloom, woke up late
and immediately blamed the sky, not enough day

in the curtains for color to be called down, his eyes
untouched by the dream-wash of windows, no radiant

rinse of reflections in sight. It's one of those mornings
he finds himself miserable because he can't think of a thing

that's his fault. He considers this while the wind outside
moves things around—intentional, no mercy, godless

as a digital clock—and the sun rushes into the room
for a few moments, brilliant, apocalyptic, firing up

the dust, banking off his money clip on its way out
of the air. Silence—night watchman no one hired,

frightened by thought, leaving by another word for light.
He considers the clouds and sun, expecting an outcome

as if he were a new kind of rain, some distant cousin
of a better flood. He doesn't get that far. He's asleep again—

naked, a new confession under his pillow. He's guilty
and doesn't care.

Daily Gods

> *Today, there are 2,700 active gods in the world.*
> *—from the Internet*

Figures the whole idea ends with the word *net*—and that's not counting what slips through the soul, lies low in our secret selves, delivery rooms of daily gods, the ones we really don't dare name. At best, language has always been a barrier between creations, expanding faster than we can train opposites. I suspect most gods would rather we say nothing, sacrifice our tongues. But saying nothing can mean something goes unanswered and answers carry the blood of afterlives, keep redefining the narrow. Statistics show 2,700 species of worm, and I've often wondered whether the figures have any special meaning, something hidden that might help calculate a looming apocalypse—the story assures us they're *earth* worms. Enter our daily gods. They know conversions are only possessions with a plan, that confessions are all that's neverending. They're aware of what's real in each of us, how the bones of personal prophets break apart, come together. They play our pipe organ of desire so well we sing along without making a sound, inching our way to some sidewalk in a heavy rain, so full of resurrection we die of it.

Staying Inside

for the Pastor

Hot. Then a pocket of air passes. Hot
again. The excitement of flies takes
center stage. Even without air their air
show goes on. Clouds resemble nothing.
Then something. The sun meets itself
on my skin. Cedars keep to themselves
more than usual, soaking their feet in
what's left of the swamp. Everyone's
telling themselves a story that begins
with *damn,* and I begin to believe certain
versions of hell as I watch the wash dry.
It's dry. Guilt emerges, confessions come
easy but always one other than my own.
Sweat keeps reminding me I might be OK
and now I'm thinking rain. If I'm perfectly
still I can hear it falling, my pores filling
up, something about to crest. My mind
thinks higher ground can make a difference
but my soul says stay put—*damn.*

Shadowing

The past is uncertain
and all that attaches him
to his bones, its tired dirt
and drift of dust the moon-
scape of his soul, no sun
strong enough to reach
a rain, no chance of something
new to name. His daughters
are gone, taken his mother
and her eyes, diluted them

with other desires. Marriage
has given up on the idea
of one, told two its endless
possibilities are impossible
to choose. Lucky for shadows,
he insists, lingering a little
longer in the shade of himself.
Only the present can survive
such a shape—it's near as a god
can come and remain one.

Signs

Pausing at a train station, breaking
from the boredom a daily jog breeds,

passing the same cracks that keep
sidewalks from crumbling, I noticed

two men holding signs—TAXI
was one in case anyone wanted

to go further. The other man held
a small deck of cards in both hands

and you had to be close to understand
what they kept repeating—AFTERLIFE

a message from a local church. Urgent.
Conditional. The promised end of all

promises. I thought about it—not going
anywhere as I watched the heat stagger

off the streets, the rails join at some
unreachable distance. I kept waiting,

letting each idea go by like the 6:45
coming to a stop at 7:21—silhouettes

in seats, mail in the last car, things
already returned unread.

Gospel

That's what happens when it happens.
—an unknown child

Not something you want
to tell your wife, say, when
you pick a night to announce
you're no longer in love
with her. With children,
however, it's something
you can gingerly turn
to song, have a church
appear in both hands,
complete with people
and steeple and doors
you can control yourself.
Your wife will want to know
more, more than you know
yourself. The only thing
that resembles magic
by then is heartbreak
and its conversion to hate.
Your hands are useless.
Your church is empty.
That's what happens,
if it happens. Next time
you're careful about believing
anything that seems to rhyme—
like hymns or sex.

Answering the Question

I was thinking
of the lizard walking
on water in the pool,
how it can snake across
a mirror or scale a wall—
yet, it couldn't find a way
out this sky-blue cell.
There it was, doomed
to die while I watched.
Of course, my friend
wouldn't let that happen
and neither would I—
she performed the rescue,
setting it free to live out
whatever was left of its tiny,
prehistoric life. Returning
to what she asked,
if I believed in the afterlife,
I said yes, without life.
I heard someone call it
The Hereafter somewhere
and something inside nodded
its bare, inside head.
She told me they were just words
and that it was either
the water or the rat terrier.
I hadn't noticed the dog,
just the lizard and how
deceptively clear it can be
to touch two surfaces
at the same time.

The Sky and I

It's the kind of sky that pulls the soul
apart, the unbeliever always first to
the eye frame, dipping the complexity
of its brush in a mixture of distance
and angle. Its art is an accuracy of light
that dissolves in the mind—appears
again, already has or will, never the same.
That's heaven. The believer, who's not
quite half, never makes it there. Its art
has too many meanings—by the time it
arrives at a canvas, all its solutions are
dry. What it sees is not what it feels.
It's not quite hell.

When I'm not here, which is where
I am now, know it's the soul you see
and not the sky. What comes to you will
only come on its own terms—the path
is longer, a scattering, scientists say.
The reds. Even as dust
we bleed.

Watching Dolphins in the Harbor with the Homeless

at Biscayne Bay

I found myself carving the silence into a shelter
and because the taste of fresh-cut timber was still

in the chair I called it home, made a street out of beach,
gave it my first name. For a few hours I lived with the windows

and doors, dreaming of something to dream of, sleeping with other eyes—
watching dolphins in the harbor with the homeless.

Home

Never mind the homeless gather cityside of the rocks,
forget how every day they stare out of the day before

like unsigned self portraits at a yard sale. Turn away
from their shoes unless you want to hear them in your

sleep one night—guest room, kitchen, pacing the pockets
of a winter coat hanging like a dead fox in a hall closet.

Pay no attention to the deceptions of a perfect fall morning
on their skin, tanned beyond tan, evidence of weather only

the air can escape without a story. Today, I'm a listener,
a thief of the bay looking for manatees to remind me myths

are always at least half true, that a sea-god still moves
in me with the strength of a starfish. A dolphin tumbles by.

The homeless have finished arriving. It's the beginning
of their day. It's the end of their day. Seaside of the rocks

salt on the homeless stiffens, their wind always northeast,
warning them home is where the heart is—warning them.

Inlet

It's where I imagine I'd go to die
if I were a baitfish all worn out

of escape. I'd simply leave the school
one day, ready myself for something

painless as perishing halfway through
a dive of my own design. Something's

always waiting, something skilled at rips
and whirlpools, capable of feigning

sunlight and shadow, gulling texture
and tone. It's why I keep coming here

to fish, hungry for what's hungry. I fish
until the inlet becomes an outlet, then

watch things go by, watch things go by
that don't go by, worn out of escape.

Current

So many different kinds without
enough power to turn the wings
of a fly. A light you can't see by
blinding you beyond darkness—
a little like a star on a night
no one's in the rip of your soul
but you, caught off guard by
someone's sudden glow of grace.
I used to think prayers carried
a kind of pulse of their own
until I realized I was receiving
everything I didn't ask for—
I'm happily poor, satisfied to eat
only what I want, and occasionally
a line comes down, incarnate,
saves me from too much positive
power, forces me to return
by heart, between beats, negative,
carrying only what's missing.

After Test Results

Anymore I seem satisfied when the day turns
quietly into the day before, eliminating the need

for weeks, months—even the years have gone
the way of paper, no mention of me. I throttle

my heart down, the travel to what I'm not slowly
turning to the horseback of desire, even bareback

on a beach of old moods. Let the beast wander,
I say—sway, hum something without words.

Dismount. The rest is by foot.

Acknowledgments

I am grateful to the following magazines in which many of these poems first appeared, often in different forms:

Barnstorm, Battered Suitcase, Bellow Literary Journal, Border Crossing, Citron Review, Chaffey Review, Foliate Oak, Gambol, Hawaii Pacific Review, IthicaLit, Jerseyworks, Kaleidoscope, L'intrique, Lunch Ticket, Medulla Review, Melusine, Montucky Review, Naugatuck River Review, New Plains Review, Oak Bend Review, Obsession, Off The Coast, OVS Magazine, Pirene's Fountain, Philadelphia Stories, Poydras, Prick of the Spindle, Sakura Review, Shadow Road Quarterly, SNReview, Thoughtsmith, Victorian Violet Journal, White Pelican Review

Cover photo by Rebecca Jean Images; author photo by Rebecca Plattner; cover and interior book design by Diane Kistner (dkistner@futurecycle.org); Chaparral Pro text with Helvetica Neue titling

About FutureCycle Press

FutureCycle Press is dedicated to publishing lasting English-language poetry and flash fiction books, chapbooks, and anthologies in both print-on-demand and ebook formats. Founded in 2007 by long-time independent editor/publishers and partners Diane Kistner and Robert S. King, the press incorporated as a nonprofit in 2012. A number of our editors are distinguished poets and authors in their own right, and we have been actively involved in the small press movement going back to the early seventies.

The FutureCycle Poetry Book Prize and honorarium is awarded annually for the best full-length volume of poetry we publish in a calendar year. We are dedicated to giving all authors we publish the care their work deserves, making our catalog of titles the most distinguished it can be, and paying forward any earnings to fund more great books.

We've learned a few things about independent publishing over the years. We've also evolved a unique, resilient publishing model that allows us to focus mainly on vetting and preserving for posterity the most books of exceptional quality without becoming overwhelmed with bookkeeping and mailing, fundraising activities, or taxing editorial and production "bubbles." To find out more about what we are doing, come see us at www.futurecycle.org.

The FutureCycle Poetry Book Prize

All full-length volumes of poetry published by FutureCycle Press in a given calendar year are considered for the annual FutureCycle Poetry Book Prize. This allows us to consider each submission on its own merits, outside of the context of a contest. Too, the judges see the finished book, which will have benefitted from the beautiful book design and strong editorial gloss we are famous for.

The book ranked the best in judging is announced as the prize-winner in the subsequent year. There is no fixed monetary award; instead, the winning poet receives an honorarium of 20% of the total net royalties from all poetry books and chapbooks the press sold online in the year the winning book was published. The winner is also accorded the honor of judging the next year's competition.

www.ingramcontent.com/pod-product-compliance
Lightning Source LLC
LaVergne TN
LVHW020938090426
835512LV00020B/3418